I'm Reading About

RHODE ISLAND

The Ocean State!

GALLOPADE

by Carole Marsh

Printed and Manufactured in Peachtree City, GA., USA
www.gallopade.com

Book design: John Hanson

Editorial manager: Janice Baker

Rhode Island is a great state.

It is one of a kind.

What makes Rhode Island special?

Let's read about it and see!

NATIVE AMERICANS

Who lived in Rhode Island first?

Native Americans did!

They moved around to find food.
They hunted in Rhode Island's woods.
They fished in Rhode Island's rivers.
They gathered fruits and seeds and nuts.

EXPLORERS

The first explorers came to Rhode Island in 1524.
They came from the country of France.

Giovanni da Verrazzano was their leader.
He and his men were trying to travel to Asia!

SETTLEMENT

A man named Roger Williams came from Massachusetts to Rhode Island.
He started the first settlement in Rhode Island.
He named it Providence.

Rhode Island was one of the original 13 colonies.

Providence

STATEHOOD

Rhode Island was the 13th state
to join the United States of America!

Isn't it great,
to be a state!
I bet Rhode Island
could hardly wait!

Rhode Island became a state in 1790.

Rhode Island
The 13th State

FLAG

I am the state flag.

What color am I?
I am white.

Look at me.
What else do you see?

I fly high over the state of Rhode Island!

HOPE

CAPITAL

Say hello to Providence,
the capital city of Rhode Island!

There is an important building in Providence.
It is the State House.
Rhode Island's laws are made there!

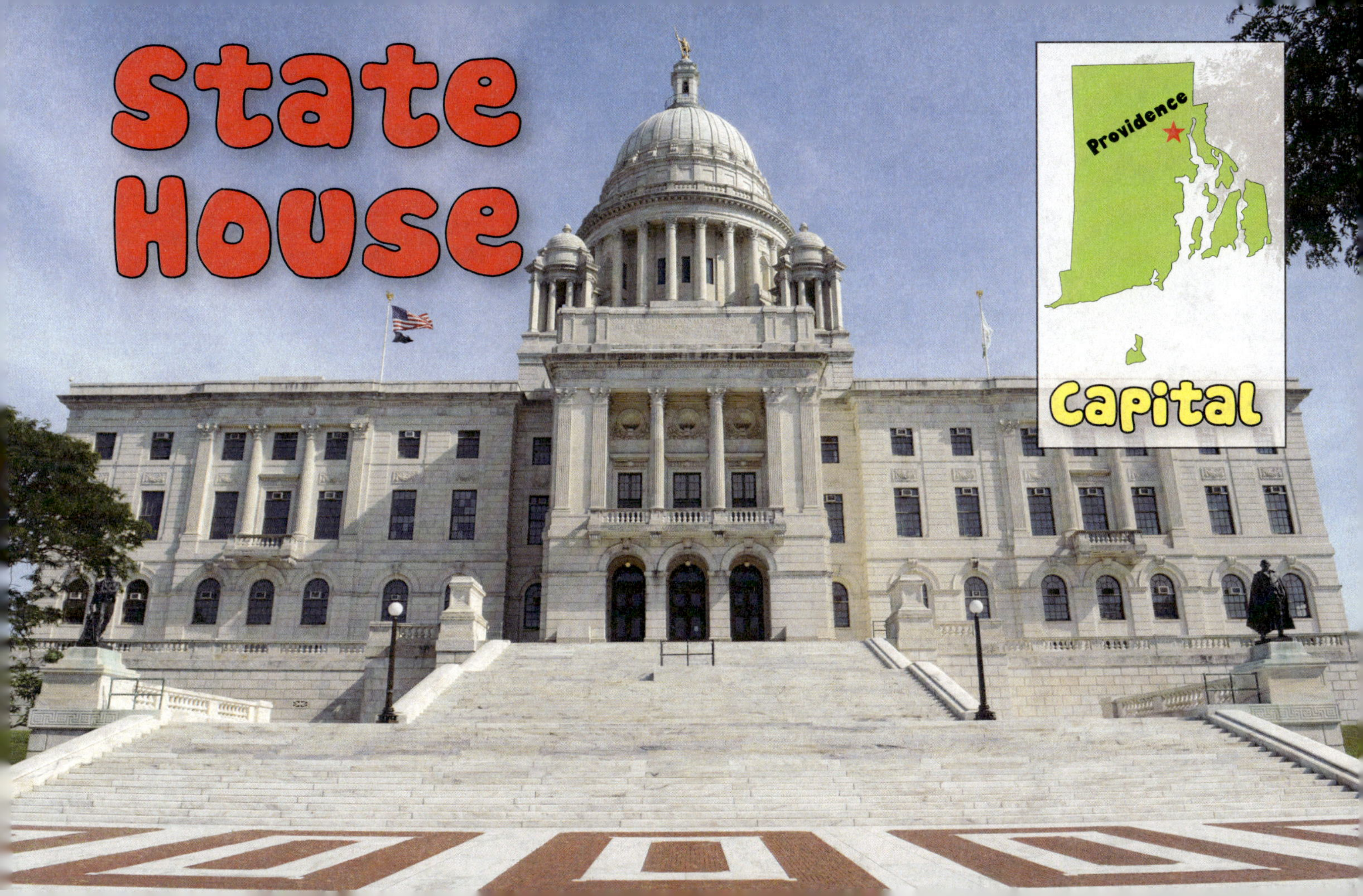
State House
Providence
Capital

SEAL

I am a seal,
but I am not the State Seal.
If I were, I would be very important.
I would be stamped on many official papers.
(Ouch, that might hurt!)

SEAL OF THE STATE OF RHODE ISLAND AND PROVIDENCE PLANTATIONS
HOPE
★ 1636 ★
Now, that's official!

NICKNAME

State nicknames are fun!
State nicknames are great!
They share fun facts
about each state!

Rhode Island's nickname is "The Ocean State."

Rhode Island's coast borders the Atlantic Ocean!

The Ocean State

BORDERS

Look at Rhode Island.
Rhode Island is in a region called "the Northeast."

Rhode Island borders two other states.
Find them on the map!

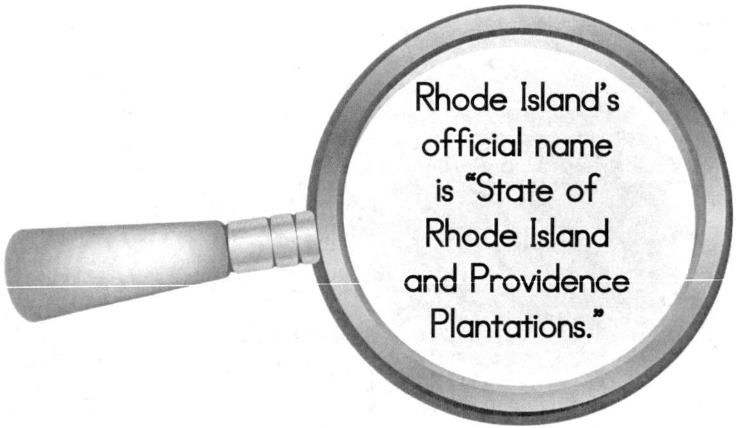

Borders

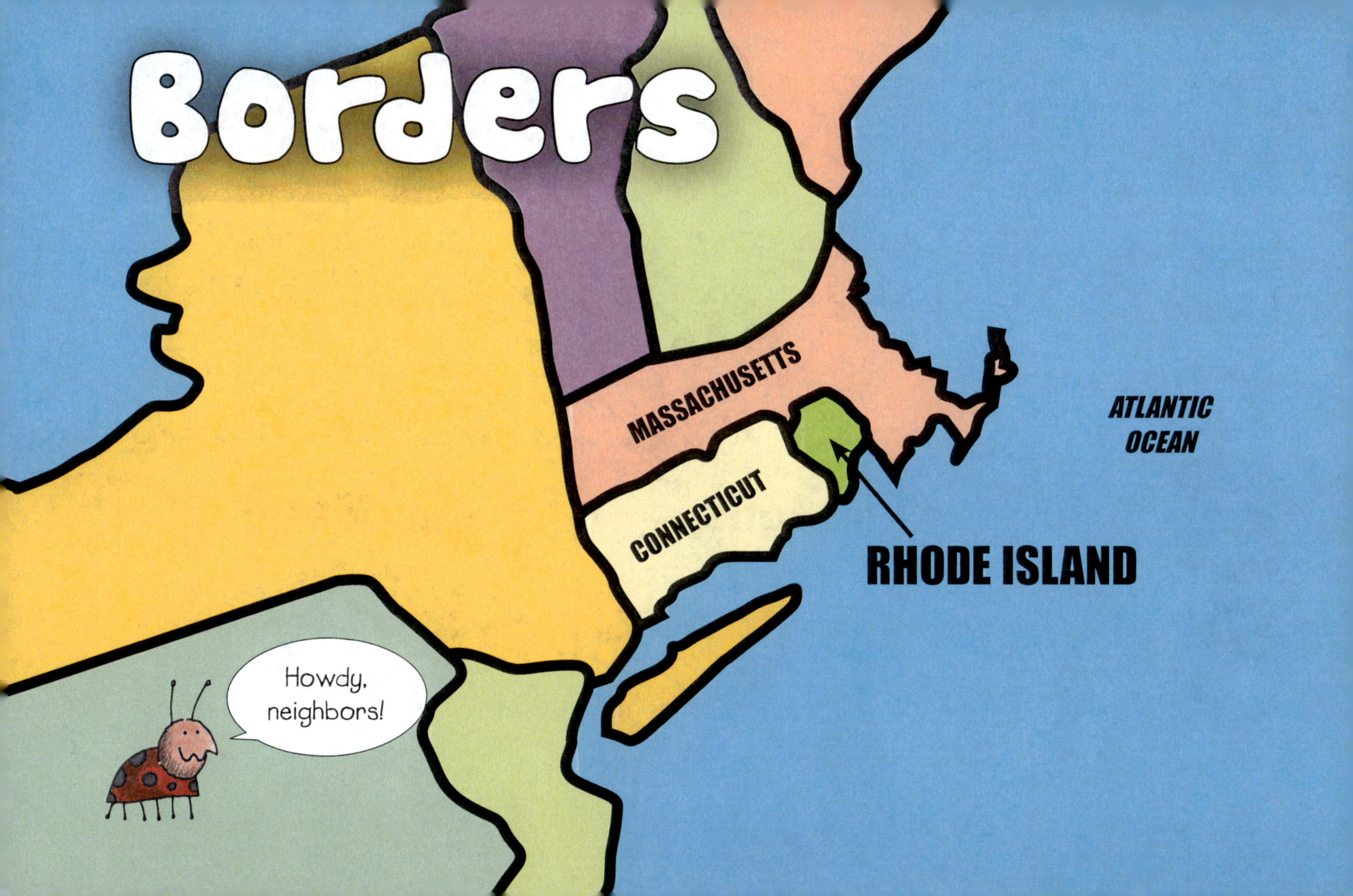
MASSACHUSETTS
CONNECTICUT
RHODE ISLAND
ATLANTIC OCEAN
Howdy, neighbors!

COUNTIES

Rhode Island is divided into five counties.
Counties are a form of local government.
Counties provide services that people need!
Those services include:

Schools **Parks** **Libraries** **Police**

Firefighters **and More!**

Counties

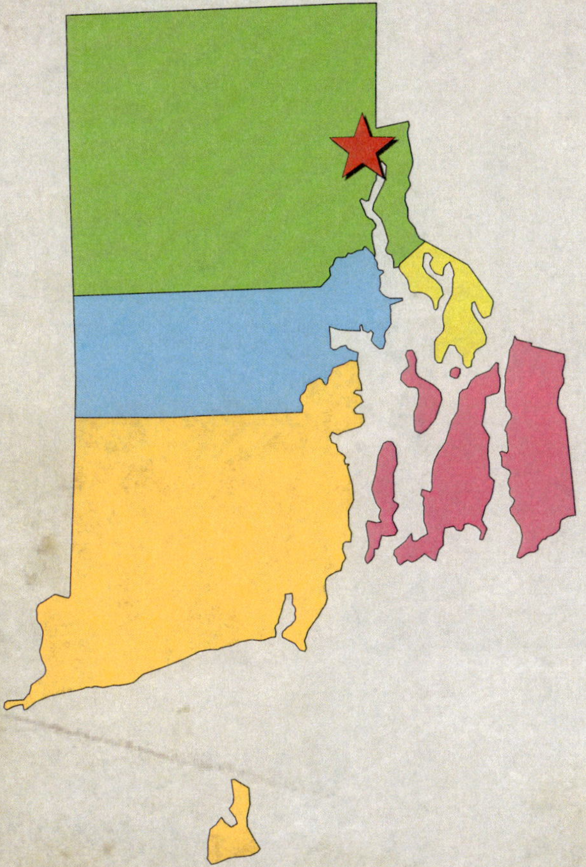

RHODE ISLAND'S CAPITAL, PROVIDENCE, IS IN PROVIDENCE COUNTY.

PEOPLE

Many famous people

Nathanael Greene

Respected general during the American Revolution

Gilbert Stuart

Artist whose painting of George Washington appears on the one-dollar bill

Samuel Slater

Known as the "Founder of the American Industrial Revolution"

call our state home!

Let's hang out!

PEOPLE

George Lima

Member of the Tuskegee Airmen, black pilots in World War II

Gina Raimondo

First female governor of Rhode Island

Elisabeth Hasselbeck

Television talk show host

Rhode Island Red

I am the state bird.
I strut and cluck around Rhode Island farms.

My feathers are fluffy.
They keep me warm.
I flap my wings to tell you "Hi!"

The Rhode Island state bird is the Rhode Island Red.

BIRD

Violet

I am the Violet.
I am the state flower.

I grow where it's warm and sunny.
I bloom in the spring and summer.
I help make Rhode Island beautiful!

Look at me! Smell me!
Schoolchildren chose me as the
state flower!

FLOWER

Red Maple

TREE

I am a Red Maple—I'm the state tree.
All over Rhode Island is where to find me.

My roots run deep, they keep me strong.
I can live for hundreds of years—that's very long!

I stand up straight, big and tall.
Don't climb too high—it would hurt to fall!

Striped Bass

I am the Striped Bass.
I am the state fish.

I swim deep in the Atlantic Ocean
off the coast of Rhode Island.

I have silver scales with black stripes.
Rhode Island fishermen like to catch me!

FISH

Atlantic Ocean

BEACHES

Let's go to the beach!

We can swim in the waves.
We can play in the sand.

We can build a big castle
where water meets land.

Rhode Island's beaches are home to many animals:

Sea Turtles **Fish** **Birds** **Crabs** **Dolphins** **and More!**

Forests

FORESTS

Rhode Island's forests are the place to be.
Hiking, fishing, camping—
fun for you and me.

Under the shade
of the tall trees,
you can see all the beautiful leaves!

Rivers

RIVERS

Rhode Island has many rivers.
People like to use rivers for boating and fishing!

This habitat is home to many animals:

Birds **Deer** **Snakes** **Frogs** **Fish** **and More!**

The Blackstone River is the longest river in Rhode Island.

Newport Mansions

LANDMARK

There are huge mansions built near the coast of Rhode Island.
They are called the Newport Mansions.
All of the mansions are more than 100 years old!
You can tour many of the mansions today.

The largest mansion is called The Breakers.
It has 70 rooms!

Rhode Island Crops

AGRICULTURE

Rhode Island has many farms.
Why?
Because Rhode Island has good soil and a mild climate!

Some of the top crops grown in Rhode Island are:

Nursery Plants **Sweet Corn** **Potatoes** **Apples**

Sports in Rhode Island

SPORTS

Baseball! Basketball! Hockey! Football!
Rhode Island has it all.

Whether you like to watch or play,
You are sure to have a ball!

Bears **Bulldogs** **Friars**

Rams

& More!

Rhode Island: The Smallest State

CLAIM TO FAME

Rhode Island is the smallest state in the United States!
It is only 48 miles long and 37 miles wide.
Rhode Island may be small, but lots of
people live there.

Rhode Island could fit inside of
Alaska almost 500 times!

GLOSSARY

climate: weather conditions in an area over a long period of time

colony: a settlement ruled by another country

habitat: a place where plants or animals naturally live

laws: rules made by the government

mansion: a very large house

nursery: place where plants are grown for sale

region: an area that has similar characteristics

scales: small, thin plates protecting the skin of fish and reptiles

settlement: the first community in an area

tour: visiting a place to look at interesting things